The Heart Contracts

poems by

Sarah Carey

Finishing Line Press
Georgetown, Kentucky

The Heart Contracts

ACKNOWLEDGMENTS

"Sinkhole" appeared in *Carolina Quarterly* (Spring 2013)
An earlier version of "Grandmother's Will" appeared in *Cottonwood* (Fall 2009)
"Upheaval" appeared in *The Portland Review* (Spring 2007)
An earlier version of "Nutritional Value" appeared in *Rattle*
"My First Steps" was a finalist in a competition sponsored by *So to Speak* (2004)
"After Dark" appeared in *Concho River Review* (Spring 2003)
An earlier version of "A Rare Disease" was published in broadsheet form by Poetry
Motel (2003.)
"The Opal Box" appeared in *Hogtown Creek Review* (Fall 2002)
"What Comes Out" appeared in *South Dakota Review* (Spring 2002)
"Climbers" and "Settlement" appeared in *The Cape Rock* (2002)
"The Heart Contracts" appeared in *Bogg* (2002)
An earlier version of "Breath" appeared in *Tule Review* (2000)
An earlier version of "The Service" appeared in *Black Buzzard Review* (1990)

Publisher: Leah Maines

Editor: Christen Kincaid

Cover Art: Raku by Tom and Nancy Giusti. Photography by Mindy Miller

Author Photo: Mindy Cherisse Miller

Cover Design: Sarah Carey and Elizabeth Maines

Printed in the USA on acid-free paper.
Order online: www.finishinglinepress.com
        also available on amazon.com

Author inquiries and mail orders:
Finishing Line Press
P. O. Box 1626
Georgetown, Kentucky 40324
U. S. A.

Table of Contents

For my parents, all of my sisters and my husband, Chad, for their unwavering support and love, and with deep gratitude to Lola Haskins for 25 years of listening, as well as for her astute editorial contributions to this work. No words can adequately express my thanks.

Because of Him

Because of him, I model
color combinations: mint and brown,
and the chocolate pumps, firm but elegant,
the bowed, trendy stilettos.

Because of him, a navy-pinstriped suit,
serious, hot, or a long linen skirt set,
black with satin seashell patches?

Because of him, I polish
a tiger eye under the cold, hard tap.

No Visible Scars

The paper said they found him
slumped over a bench at midnight
dirt-haired, hazel eyes glazed
in blue jeans, white shirt, tennis shoes
no visible scars or tattoos.

It hit me hard when I heard
of the murder. He was halfway to Tallahassee
where he grew up in the block house
on a side street off Magnolia, near Indian Head.

When Robert died his sister cried
for the guest bed, but our trust was gone
although we'd let go of the ring
she stole from Mother years ago.

In the restaurant parking lot
cops still comb for evidence. He was beaten, we read
but what I know is he hitched sober
from Miami to the bus stop
where he slept before he died,
stretched out beneath the stars.

—For Robert Leigh

Max

When I bought him
my fears disappeared, my sleep returned.
He grew to eat at all hours

cheese and dirt and wood,
the legs of my poplar cabinet
turned to putty and to this day

the thought of him makes me weak.
No children for me
all those years, only his kiss.

What would he want?
Steak fat, ginger snaps.
The last piece of cheesecake.

I'm thin now, but cut away
there's still no joy.
When I feel the world is beige

or shudder at dark news,
I remember how he redefined off-white,
his brown hairs recoverable only with tape

from the overstuffed couch.
How bright the world became then,
how full! When I pull his collar from storage

it reeks from sweet and sour
but I can't put it away,
its cracked leather so like a second skin.

Budget Class

I never did know how to ask for money.
In a fight with my monitor,

both of us blink. Finally
I clear the prompts

and find the drop-down menu
to select my funds.

I collect my thoughts
about what matters:

Travel. Supplies. Dues,
perhaps a miscellaneous reserve.

These are projects that have come
and gone, empty cells for jobs

I know too well are pending.
I see the ledger has no line

for blood. The more I ask for,
the more I have to explain.

Evaluation

Lock door, clear desk
except for spreadsheets,

send calls to voice mail.
Recall a year in lists:

how many stories written,
how wide ranging, the collateral.

Explain how implementation
of marketing plan purloined core duties,

note the thrill of growing
in the job, the new technology.

Justify how much I'm worth.
I stop and start, the way I always do.

After we talk, nothing will change.
Not what I did. Not who I am, or will be.

I begin again, rearrange my tenses.

The Gift

I've pulled the Blenko vase out
for display, to soak up sun
wherever it might play, on graceful shoulders

or those sultry pitcher lips. It came
with all best wishes, packed in peanuts
I remember to this day

the way Cobalt took up residence
alongside tarnished silver, impractical trays,
made friends with earth-toned greenware,

never stayed in one place too long
nor hid its museum grace.

Today I read a blog post of her death,
am powerless now to say the Blenko
never broke or chipped, never held daffodils.

I move it from its temporary resting place,
consoled to see the evening light reflect.

A Rare Disease

We work backwards:
who did what to whom, who took which drug
for pain? We chart ways of birth control
from pills to foam, to finally, withdrawal.
Cross the what-ifs off our lists.
Who else might we have exposed?
Who yet might learn from our mistakes?

We share which lines in our respective genes
could predispose us to this end,
exercise our possibilities, not excited,
not content, not with the long view of regret
but rather with the fixed eyes of predators
biding our time, tracking blood scent,
having set about to kill doubt
and, if we're lucky, pinpoint how to live.

Nutritional Value

Someone has a feeding tube
removed while I'm eating my Cobb
at Friday's, thinking green is good this time
of year, since last evening's leftover pot roast
will send me over my quota of red

meat, the vitamins of carrots and potatoes
diminished after hours of simmer.
But oh, don't forget the bleeding
of flavors, the tenderness
of shoulder falling from bone.

My First Steps

Inside the house I bought at 34
a pine secretary perfects a corner.
A poplar chest completes a wall,
beneath the crown molding

as if it had been there forever.
It opened from the front
like your gown so many years ago
when I learned your buttons.

You were my first visitor, loving my woods.
It's June again, new graduates
pack restaurants, tube the Ichetucknee.

Now, as then, we stay in,
rearrange my pieces room by room
by story, like when the washer hose broke
and I rose to inch-thick puddles

ran next door for a neighbor,
who shut off the valve.
Mother, my Hestia, my sacrifice
is for whatever you cultivate in me:

what I had to gut to get
to what just now and finally
feels right, like confessing how I cried all night
on the ruined Berber when Max died.

—For Sally Malloy

Pattern Maker

Vouched-for German William John,
arrived in Indiana in the 1920s,
an apprentice molding a new life
at Wayne Pump. He built two houses
side by side on Berry Street
with a yard full of cherries, night crawlers.

My father slumped into depression
when he died. I was teen-aged,
chasing boys and acting out
another grief when Dad left home again
to trace my great-grandfather's steps
from birth in Mecklenburg
to the church where as a young man

he met Mary Hamm, domestic
to a British admiral. With his own new bride,
my father walked, he had to move
the way one does when one is young,
and strong, spring in his step

spurred to witness and intent
to put his eyes where William John's hands
had been, those master pattern maker hands,
so many years ago, bundled well
against a bitter wind, walked street by street
and light by light to find their names
scrawled in the marriage record.

—For John Carey

Grandmother's Will

Forget the time it took, day in
day out, to warm supper,
schedule the help, to quell doubts
you were who you said you were.

When you signed for her, I saw
how time steals legibility,
how she lost the will or hid it,
saw sun specks on her wrists,

the purple flecked topography of veins
in the slim legs you inherited
and I did not. How transparent
I've become in my desire to stay young.

I'm a grinder, says my dentist.
You could say what needed to be said
and sleep at night. I dreamt of freeing
whatever was stuck on the roof.

At the fountain where the girls went
in Mt. Gilead, I imagine Grandmother's black hair,
her white shoulders leaning to the men
who drank in her shadows.

She was beautiful, alone. Then you came
and she shone. You always knew
her letting go would come

without fanfare. On her birthday
when I ask you if you think of her,
you say finally, *not with sadness, no.*

The Brightest Star

Like an impatient guest, Quiet taps
taps taps TAPS

then body blows
open the door

and Grief flows in.
Outside, a gibbous moon

reflects over the vast Atlantic.
Outside, Jupiter rises in the east.

We stare and strain, as if to see
the brightest star could set us free.

He liked the moon, we remember. He would say, "Did you see the moon?"
         —For John Malloy, 1929-2011

The Conch

We strolled Panhandle beaches
where you'd never see a car. Chased sinking
coquinas, whole sand dollars, the occasional starfish.

Always a crush underfoot, this was home
and home was not caring how we looked
or who said what to whom, in the dunes,

in too-brief hiatuses from growing up.
In my fifties, I seek refuge Atlantic-side
when I can get away, tread lightly barefoot,

having been cut before. A conch presents itself
intact — a rarity. I pick it up and I'm inside
the roar the shell, lifted, makes.

Upheaval

There I was like Prufrock on a pin,
floor-sprawled, blood spilling
into tissue in my wrist, a process
I knew well by then:

broken wine glass, bruise,
when purple skin segues to blue
then into yellow, when healing begins.
I willed myself up. My life sank in.

It's been months since the fall.
Close to shore, falcate fins break our fields
of vision, now and then a fluke.
My husband sees inverse of crash,

forgiving depths of water. I in turn
see barbs of rays and threat
but will say this: I'm motivated
to stay dry. The sun declines,
makes abalone iridescence of bottlenose.

Sinkhole

We head for the sinkhole that just opened up
in the neighborhood, a bit of news, not on a par
with the rapist's arrest, but still news, so we cross
the main drag, listen for sirens.

A father and son in the distance
stalk past variegated flax lilies
fresh in the ground, perfect piles
of debris next to overgrown grass.

We pass the for-sale sign near the corner house
rounded so many times, keep going
out of habit. After ambling the circle,
her business complete, the dog pulls
toward the karst, as if to refocus our intent
past predictable points to the downpour's
new pond, past projection to absorb
the undulating bass chords of frogs.

Soon it's dark, too late to make
the gaping scene, so we turn for home
back up the trail with our old dog,
who moves slowly, nosing sky and mulch

an animal's scent in the woods, rain smells
while the water's weight accumulates,
limestone sinks and the ground caves,
foot by footfall, drop by drop.

Neuropathies

That month, neuropathies stole the show
the totaled car in the last snow
from the 10-foot-high embankment
from which a father/husband/friend walked away.
I saw them skating
on the edge, heroes in the pictures
I had formed of them,
extremity being the Alaskan way.

Soon, though, the tingling started,
first in one foot, then the other,
then in his fingers, his linebacker legs.
He says he burns, buries his hands
in his pockets. Now I notice tremors,

his faltering penmanship in the book of poems
he inscribed in memory of my visit,
his nerves no home alarm
could sway. He steels himself,
ticks up the recliner to watch the game.
We settle in for the final quarter.

Kites

In front of us, the surfers' kites
break darkening sky. Farther from shore
two paddle hard against the riptides,
to ride the surf back in.

We speak the yin and yang of beach
in our own familiar tongue and groove
moving through our last vacation walk.
This time we listen less

to each other, more to sand squeaking
beneath our feet, to currents
sweeping away lost faces

then releasing them to blow back in
as a giant wave, or tears.

Cows Keening

Across miles of fence, the keening carried
from the pasture west of our back yard
from cows whose moos soothed us
in our new house.

Our home felt like a ranch,
we told our Utah relatives.
There were coyotes, cows
a family of owls.

When my husband said,
"They must have taken the calves,"
I knew how much I'd never know,
their bellows echoing in the black night.

Baby Shower

For the first time in twenty years,
our masks wash away. Time melts,

I can't say why. Perhaps that year of chemo
or the mountain in Maine summited

afterwards. Maybe to hear finally
what only you could tell me of fading careers,

the old people. We move closer
in the rented chairs inside the sunroom.

In front of us, the young guests blend
in a room overflowing with bags

full of tissue, reuseable bows.

After Dark

Hot wires rev the engine to life.
A man's car for fifteen years
roars out of a familiar driveway
for the last time.

Discovering the empty garage
the next morning, the owner
walks to work, missing the worn
seats, the fresh paint

a woman he took in the rear
before the smell of dog took over
at two hundred thousand highway miles,
the second set of shocks.

Soon it hits the man. He was upstairs,
snoring to the heavens
when the dogs barked, waking the neighbors.
He dreamed on, oblivious

to the world of thieves.
It doesn't dawn on him yet
to feel relief he did not hear, no,
or act, instead he feels guilty

for his absence from the crime,
as if he asked for it, leaving the car
unlocked, believing in the good neighborhood,
breathing conditioned air in his sleep.

The Heart Contracts

Max leans his jaw forward into my hand
from the folded-down back seat,
watches the country drive,
the trees race by. From his perspective
someone else is in control.

Minutes later his head falls
on the plain, white sheet.
It will happen to us all, eventually,
I know. He is old, but it is not time, it is just
not time, and it is just not just.

Taking him back to the hospital
my gyrations evolve from lists:
What has happened since the medicine?
Am I moving fast enough
from Point A to Point B?
"Honey, won't you help me move the cage,
he travels better in it." Push, heave.

I am unable to bring anything
to its logical conclusion.

Now and then bright eyes in the rearview
betray a reprieve: Days later
he'll return to chasing crows,
I think, returning to upbeat.
In this dream, routine returns.
I let him go, squeeze myself tight.

In a few hours, in what seems a lifetime
Max and I go home, we live, we love

and in between, I believe.

The Opal Box

It comes down, the clerk says,
from across a felt box
full of pendants, to whether
I am a symmetrical
or an asymmetrical person,

which particular synthetic,
that is to say, fake Australian opal
would be best for me,
dangling from my neck.
Considering all the options,

I think, really, there is just
no question, although the absence
of authenticity in this case
means the risk of stepping out
is more affordable somehow,

more allowable, an investment
in some artist's freeform answer
to inhibition. No question when push
comes to shove, I will always
choose that perfect center

safe love to square me away,
no question that the unnatural fire exploding
blues and purples deeper than illusion
draws me to this point, ready to pay
the 14 carat consequences, letting a stranger

weigh the gold to offer me his best price
on both simulated stones,
and just for that short time,
even knowing what I know,
I hang in that balance.

Breath

Take Mozart, born for kings
and variations, the reach and slide
of the 40th symphony.

Or Monet in London, cycling in
and out of weather,
measuring his days in light.

How a body depends.
How waves break with dawn
drawing the white caps past the shoreline.

What follows fire,
the grinning death.
What comes after the sun, the moon.

The wren that suddenly makes its night home
in the air plant, what flowers
throwing off seeds, then decays in wetness

What comes into your right heart
as mere blood, then pumps its way out
as spirit, stops, if you listen,

then starts again, knowing just how far back,
how deep to go, hugging your throat,
kissing your lips goodbye, hello.

Climbers

A certain stream's reputation
draws us out and up.

We climb the occasional promontory,
look out over the town,

the highest hills,
over someone's reservations.

One in our group was fired,
one is having an affair. I personally peaked

last year on drama but am ready now
on all counts for a raise.

Perhaps the air carries our voices,
sharing views, driving a point.

Whose first book will be taken
by the best house, whose memoir?

The clearly contrasting approach,
a running argument. The next step

overcomes the rush ahead.
In no time, only our boots

will remember the flat earth.

Settlement

The new owner puts in crossties,
ten, maybe twelve feet into the limerock,
deepening beneath a layer of red clay.

Soon after the closing, cracks
in the second-floor ceiling congeal.
Whatever you look up to is seamless.

Marvel how the roof held as long as it did,
how the termites never came.
As for your own endurance,
it feels good to wave away geography

imagine the wall to be torn down
the etched-glass pane that will stand
in its place, facing the hallway.
The openness a stranger will wake to.

You can only guess
if the newcomers will stay longer,
sleep better when the heavy rains come
on dark nights, cry out less

leaving the foundation of your concerns
to trail you to the next house and the next
like a restless ghost, that piece of your past
you can't leave, shed or bury

that won't fade or forgive, that wants most
of all to forget, let go, but knows
that will never in this life be possible.

The Service

A small silver box. A woman,
bent in a folding chair. A guitar.
The smell of roses greets us
along with the man in black disbursing programs

most will not see to read, their eyes
bleeding a world of hope in one short life,
in pieces as they dab and dry.
It could have been theirs,

this short service. Hand-outs with words
to the one song the dead child loved,
clapping his thumb-sized hands with glee.
There was a babe in all of us

we sing for and give up.
The box descends.
Childless, I rise.

What Comes Out

He appreciates the new Cuban diner,
the hot fudge smell on Duval Street
though it is always a struggle
—learning to speak in the Key West tongue
getting here, training to overcome
that Utah fear of water. Let's go out on a boat
I said. As usual, he went along.

Alone in this waterfront café, I order.
It is straightforward, what I want:
the best I ever had, served yesterday.
Just bring it to me again
I say. Something tells me it was not
the bacon (whole pieces not bits)
or blue cheese (chunky not crumbled)
not even the mesquite-grilled chicken
falling apart at the fork.
It was the medley that left me
not just full, but believing
this could just be something
I would never tire of.

What he feels in water, he has learned
to minimize. Only I know he will dive
in a lake much closer to home,
and only with me. I am with him now
washing the dishes. After dinner
when he turns the bed down,
I am in his mouth.
It is who I was that he remembers.

Today the luncheon Cobb has a fresh
shaving of carrots. There is something tart
about the dressing, the rare meat.
It is all I ever wanted.

A North Carolina native, Sarah Carey grew up in Florida, where she has lived most of her life. After two years at Duke University, Sarah finished her undergraduate education at Florida State University, where she majored in political science and began taking creative writing classes. While in college, Sarah co-edited FSU's literary publication, *Sundog* (now *Southeast Review*) and served on the board of directors for the Tallahassee Writer's Co-op. She received a master's degree in English from FSU with a concentration in creative writing in 1981.

One of the poems from her creative thesis was a finalist in the Academy of American Poets competition and in the final year of her graduate program, Sarah had her first poetry publication in the Florida Review. In the years since, she has received several awards at the contest level for her work and has continued to publish poems in a variety of small magazines and literary journals.

After completing her graduate studies, Sarah began working for weekly newspapers in the Florida Panhandle. In 1990, she began working for the University of Florida College of Veterinary Medicine, where she remains today as director of public relations. Her work has received several awards from the Florida Public Relations Association, which named her its Jack M. Detweiler Professional of the Year in 2012.

She lives in Gainesville with her husband, Chad Hunsaker, and their black Labrador retriever, Finn.

www.ingramcontent.com/pod-product-compliance
Lightning Source LLC
LaVergne TN
LVHW041329080426
835513LV00008B/644